HOMEGROWN TERROR
THE OKLAHOMA CITY BOMBING

Victoria Sherrow

 Enslow Publishers, Inc.
40 Industrial Road
Box 398
Berkeley Heights, NJ 07922
USA

http://www.enslow.com

Original edition published as *The Oklahoma City Bombing: Terror in the Heartland* in 1998.

Library of Congress Cataloging-in-Publication Data
Sherrow, Victoria.
   Homegrown terror : the Oklahoma City bombing / Victoria Sherrow.
      p. cm. — (Disasters—people in peril)
   "Original edition published as The Oklahoma City Bombing: Terror in the Heartland in 1998."
   Includes bibliographical references and index.
   Summary: "Examines the Oklahoma City Bombing, including the events of April 19, 1995; stories from witnesses, survivors, and rescue workers; the perpetrators behind the terrorist attack and the aftermath of the tragedy"—Provided by publisher.
   ISBN 978-0-7660-4016-8
   1. Oklahoma City Federal Building Bombing, Oklahoma City, Okla., 1995—Juvenile literature. 2. Terrorism—Oklahoma—Oklahoma City—Juvenile literature. 3. Bombing investigation—Oklahoma—Oklahoma City—Juvenile literature. I. Sherrow, Victoria. Oklahoma City bombing. II. Title.
   HV6432.S53 2013
   363.32509766'38—dc23

                   2011050738

Future editions:
Paperback ISBN 978-1-4644-0107-7
ePUB ISBN 978-1-4645-1014-4
PDF ISBN 978-1-4646-1014-1

Printed in the United States of America
032012 Lake Book Manufacturing, Inc., Melrose Park, IL
10 9 8 7 6 5 4 3 2 1

To Our Readers: We have done our best to make sure all Internet addresses in this book were active and appropriate when we went to press. However, the author and the publisher have no control over and assume no liability for the material available on those Internet sites or on other Web sites they may link to. Any comments or suggestions can be sent by e-mail to comments@enslow.com or to the address on the back cover.

♻ Enslow Publishers, Inc., is committed to printing our books on recycled paper. The paper in every book contains 10% to 30% post-consumer waste (PCW). The cover board on the outside of each book contains 100% PCW. Our goal is to do our part to help young people and the environment too!

Illustration Credits: AP Images / Amy Sancetta, p. 28; AP Images / Beth A. Keiser, p. 26; AP Images / Bill Waugh, p. 1; AP Images / *The Daily Oklahoman*, Jim Argo, p. 4; AP Images / *The Daily Oklahoman*, Paul Hellstern, p. 7; AP Images / David Longstreath, pp. 8, 10, 15, 16, 24, 31; AP Images / David J. Phillip, p. 18; AP Images / David Zalubowski, p. 40; AP Images / Greg Smith, p. 21; AP Images / Gulnara Samoilova / PA Wire URN: 5244504, p. 39; AP Images / J. Pat Carter, p. 13; AP Images / Jeff Mitchell, p. 34; AP Images / Jerry Laizure, p. 32; AP Images / Sue Ogrocki, p. 37.

Cover Illustration: AP Images / Bill Waugh (Thousands of people attend a memorial service in front of the Alfred P. Murrah Federal Building in Oklahoma City on May 5, 1995).

CONTENTS

A firefighter walks by explosion-damaged cars near the smoldering ruins of the Alfred P. Murrah Federal Building in Oklahoma City on April 19, 1995. The bomb that decimated the building could be heard from miles around.

CHAPTER ONE

"THIS ISN'T SUPPOSED TO HAPPEN"

IT WAS UNFORGETTABLE—the booming noise that pierced the air in Oklahoma City on the morning of April 19, 1995. A ball of flame rose toward the sky. Within seconds, the front of the nine-story Alfred P. Murrah Federal Building had crumbled to the ground. A quiet spring day had become a living nightmare.

The bomb that devastated this building resounded for miles around. People within thirty miles of the city heard the noise and felt a tremor. Melva Noakes was working at a day care center in Choctaw, twenty miles from Oklahoma City. She remembered, "We went outside and saw a jet and thought [the explosion] must have been a sonic boom."[1] Some people thought the noise was thunder. They saw lights flash in the sky and wondered why lightning had struck on a clear day.

What had struck was a van loaded with nearly 4,800 pounds of explosives. In that instant, 168 lives were cut short. Thousands of other people were left injured or grieving.

Some people inside the federal building survived the initial blast. One of them was Michael Reyes. His office was on the seventh floor. Reyes recalled what happened that Wednesday morning:

> I was sitting at my desk, and I had just gotten off the phone and then the power went off. And that was a weird sensation because the power had never gone off. And then I started hearing this rumbling, and I guess I thought it was an earthquake. I thought, "I need to get under my desk" and then I looked at my desk. It was just shaking violently like it was going to break apart.[2]

Michael Reyes crouched under his desk. Then, suddenly, the floor gave way. He said, "I started to fall—but I was in a dive. And I thought, 'I'm just going to fall down seven floors and that's going to be it—it's just going to be over."[3]

On the third floor, staff members of the federal credit union office were holding a meeting. They were seated around the desk of director Florence Rogers. As the bomb exploded, Rogers saw eight of her fellow employees plunge through the floor and into the ground.

Scientists would later explain that when the bomb went off, super-hot gas had streaked through the building at a speed of 8,000 feet per second. "Those standing out front were slammed with a force equal to 37 tons. One man, they said, who was taking a cigarette break outdoors, was vaporized into the wall."[4]

An instant later, the gas evaporated. A fierce vacuum formed. "Oxygen was sucked out of the air. The ground shook as if it were being tossed by a full-scale earthquake."[5]

This mighty explosion tore apart the federal building and sent glass and concrete flying onto the streets. Scattered in the dust and debris were children's toys. It was a dreadful reminder that a day care center had been operating inside the building. That morning, parents had

Firefighters search through rubble for survivors on the fifth floor of the Alfred P. Murrah Federal Building in Oklahoma City a day after the deadly bombing attack.

Relatives and police console an unidentified woman after she learned that her child was trapped in the day care center at the **Alfred P. Murrah Federal Building.** After the explosion, people rushed to the bomb site to provide assistance and search for their loved ones.

arrived with their children as usual. Among them were A. C. Cooper and his wife, Dana, the director of the center. A.C. had dropped off Dana and their two-year-old son, Anthony Christopher, then kissed them good-bye. It was the last time he would see them alive.

After the explosion, people from around Oklahoma City rushed to the bomb site to help. Black smoke swirled around them. Cars had been blown to pieces and parking meters were knocked down. Glass and concrete lay strewn along the sidewalks.

Among those who hurried to the site was Dolores Watson. Her grandson, P. J. Allen, had been in the day care center. Watson later said, "When I looked at that building, I didn't—I couldn't imagine anyone coming out alive out of that building."[6]

As they arrived, police, firefighters, and rescue workers were visibly upset. Assistant Fire Chief Jon Hansen said, "This isn't supposed to happen in the heartland."[7]

Survivors injured during the bombing attack at the Alfred P. Murrah Federal Building gather near the explosion site to receive medical attention. As dazed victims emerged from the building, doctors, nurses, police officers, and many others were there to help.

CHAPTER TWO

HOURS OF AGONY

AS RESCUE TEAMS ARRIVED, stunned survivors were emerging from the ruins of the bombed building. They were terribly wounded and burned. Others had no shoes, and their clothing hung in shreds. Some people had lost an eye, an arm, a leg, or fingers.

From the rubble, police and firefighters heard children crying. They hurried toward the sounds to find survivors. Police sergeant John Avera recalled, "We started moving bricks and rocks and we found two babies."[1] Medics gently wrapped the severely burned, barely living infants in white gauze.

In the face of this disaster, people came to help. There were medical and nursing students, off-duty police officers, clergy, engineers, and others. One hundred physicians from Oklahoma City had gone to a medical conference in Houston. When they heard about the bombing, they flew back home.

Stephen Pruitt was one of the injured. He was thrown against a brick wall so hard that he had brick prints on his skin. His nose was broken and his eye was severely injured. Luckily, his injuries were less severe than those of some others.

Michael Reyes had fallen down four stories to the third floor. He was still conscious but badly cut and bruised. People who worked on that floor lowered him to ground level. From there, medics placed him on a stretcher.

Reyes asked about his father, who worked in another part of the building. Nobody could find him. In ten days, the family would find out that Michael's father had died. His office was in the worst-hit part of the building.

People outside the federal building also suffered severe injuries. Candy Avey had parked her car and was entering the building when the bomb went off. She says, "I was blown back, wrapped around the meter, and my face hit the car."[2] Avey suffered a broken arm and jaw. She described another victim who was entering the building: "His arm was blown off. But he was in such shock that he didn't even notice it. He just kept on going, attempting to help others around him."[3]

Flying glass caused many injuries, including punctured lungs. Nurse Shirley Moser said, "When you see what it does, you can't believe it. It's as though you filled a shotgun shell with slivers of glass and shot it at someone."[4]

Polly Nichols worked across the street at the *Journal Record* building. Flying glass struck her in the throat and severely sliced two major

An unidentified victim of the bombing attack is helped from the scene. People who had been outside the building also suffered severe injuries from the impact of the explosion and flying glass.

blood vessels. Nichols stumbled down a flight of stairs and then collapsed. A coworker carried her outside where a doctor quickly got her into an ambulance. She later told reporter Wade Goodwyn, "I came within 10 minutes of dying."[5]

Dan Webber worked in an office in the courthouse down the street from the federal building. The force of the explosion threw him across the room. But Webber was much more upset by the fact that his three-year-old son, Joseph, was at the day care center. He raced down the street to his wife's office. Together, they ran to the bomb site and searched frantically for their son.

Twenty minutes later, a policeman walked by with Joseph in his arms. He was cut and bleeding, with a broken arm and ruptured eardrums. But the Webbers were overjoyed to find their child alive.

Dolores Watson's grandson P. J. was also found alive. He suffered burns and a fracture.

Two of the most distraught people at the bomb site were Jim Denny, a fifty-year-old toolmaker, and his wife, Claudia. Their two children, two-year-old Rebecca and three-year-old Brandon, were at the day care center. Denny was stunned when he saw the smoking ruins of the federal building. He later said, "I thought a nine-story building had disappeared."[6]

The Dennys rushed to a Red Cross center to wait for news of their children. A local news station reported that an unidentified little girl with long, red hair was in surgery at Southwest Medical Center. It was Rebecca Denny. She had serious cuts and burns, but doctors said she would eventually recover.

Where was Brandon? Hours later, the Dennys heard that a boy with reddish-blond hair was at Presbyterian Hospital. Inside the former day care center, Brandon was found covered in the dust and debris. His rescuer recalled, "I cradled [him] in my arms and noticed that he had a head injury and appeared to have a brick sticking out of his forehead. The boy was holding a little green block."[7]

Claudia Denny holds her son, Brandon, at their home in south Oklahoma City on March 22, 1996. Rebecca Denny is sitting behind them. Both children suffered severe injuries in the day care center when the bomb detonated.

Flying debris had torn a hole in Brandon's skull. He would remain in critical condition for several days. However, his parents felt they had experienced two miracles that day.

For other parents, there were no miracles. Only six of the children in the day care center survived. Rescue workers found the body of child care worker Wanda Howell. She was holding two-year-old Dominique London, also dead, in her arms. Four infants had been resting in cribs located near the front of the building. They died at once. Four children outside the center also died. They had been visiting the federal building the day of the bombing.

Malissa McNeely recalled the moment that she heard about the bombing. She said, "I broke out in a frenzy, crying and shaking. I got the kids in the car and went downtown."[8] As a working mother, McNeely usually left her two children at the center. This was her day off and she had kept the children home. However, she knew that her sister's only child, Tony, was there. Tony died in the bombing.

Thu Nguyen and his wife were among those who waited fearfully at the Children's Hospital. Their five-year-old son, Christopher, had been at the day care center. Now he was in surgery. An outraged Nguyen said, "I've seen war, O.K.? I've seen soldiers I fought with in Vietnam. . . . That was war. These are children. This is not a war. This is a crime."[9]

Many people wept when they saw a picture of firefighter Chris Fields holding the limp, bloodied body of Baylee Almon. Baylee had celebrated her first birthday the day before the bombing.

Baylee's grieving mother said, "I know my daughter is in heaven. I know she is."[10]

Oklahoma City District Fire Chief Mike Shannon, one of the first to arrive on scene following the terrorist attack, searches through the ruins of the Alfred P. Murrah building. The bombing killed 168 people, including 19 children, and left many more injured.

CHAPTER THREE

HOPE AND DESPAIR

OFFICIALS PLEDGED TO KEEP SEARCHING for any survivors. One woman standing near the site told reporters, "There's still hope. I've just been telling them to keep praying."[1]

As rescue teams pressed on, volunteers arrived. Donors lined up at Red Cross centers to give blood. Local restaurants supplied pizza, hamburgers, and other food to rescue crews, volunteers, and victims' families. People arrived with carloads of baby formula, flashlights, food, clothing, and other things. A sporting goods store in Stillwater, Oklahoma, shipped boxes of knee pads for the rescue workers.[2]

A team of sixty firefighters from Phoenix, Arizona, arrived soon after the bombing. They were experts at recovering bodies from rubble. By afternoon, it was clear that dozens of people were dead. Chief Phil Yeager of the Phoenix Fire Department told reporters: "It's absolutely a race against time in slow motion. We have searched every area that you can just walk up to and search. Now it's a matter of getting into those

Rescue crews work together as they climb over debris in search of victims a day after the deadly bombing attack in Oklahoma City. Despite the dangerous conditions of the unstable building, rescue workers did not give up the search for survivors.

very dangerous, very unstable areas. . . . The possibility that there may be just one person in there is what keeps you going."[3]

In the fight to save lives, rescuers in hard hats used hydraulic saws to break up concrete. Cranes lifted large chunks of debris. Dogs sniffed the debris to locate bodies, dead or alive. One person found alive that first day was Priscilla Sayers. For nearly five terrifying hours, Sayers had lain buried, praying.

Heavy winds arose, making rescue work harder. During the afternoon, workers were told to halt. Officials feared the building might collapse. But that evening, the struggle resumed. Giant spotlights were beamed onto the area.

A group of rescuers was thrilled to find twenty-year-old Daina Bradley. She was trapped in the basement. Her body lay beneath cement girders and a steel bar that was holding up heavy parts of the building. The firefighters knew they must use extreme care to remove the debris or tons of concrete could fall on her.

Dr. Gary Massad was one of the doctors who stayed with this victim among the debris. He watched nervously as Bradley's blood pressure dropped below normal. He later said, "My greatest fear was that I would be ordered to leave the building, that I would have to leave her trapped there."[4]

The men decided to cut the steel bar so they could reach Bradley. One of her legs was totally crushed. Doctors agreed that they must cut it off below the knee to save her life. They faced another dilemma. Giving Bradley too many painkillers could send her into a coma. She endured immense pain as doctors cut off her leg and freed her from the debris. Later, her rescuers learned that Bradley's mother and her two children had died in the bombing.

Was anyone else alive? As the night wore on, people began to lose hope. Among those who refused to give up were Dr. Rick Nelson and six colleagues. They had come as volunteers from a hospital in Muskogee, Oklahoma. Suddenly, at about 10:00 P.M., Nelson heard someone shout, "We've got a live one!"[5]

A rescue dog had found a foot. It belonged to fifteen-year-old Brandy Liggons. Nelson said, "She was completely covered in rubble, twisted metal . . . of about two inches in diameter. She seemed to be wrapped around a metal chair."[6]

Slowly and carefully, workers removed the heavy objects that trapped Liggons. They tried not to cause further injuries. Dr. Nelson held Liggons's hand and gave her oxygen. He talked and joked to keep up her spirits during the three-hour rescue. Finally, she was brought out and placed in an ambulance. During surgery, her injured spleen was removed. Liggons survived, despite bruised lungs and other injuries. Nelson said, "That girl's a miracle."[7]

While she was in the hospital, Brandy Liggons had a very famous visitor: talk show host and actress Oprah Winfrey. Winfrey said she was inspired by Liggons's courage. She told her, "Brandy, if you can survive this, you can survive anything."[8]

Brandy Liggons was the last survivor found. All during the night and the next day, terrified families waited anxiously at the Red Cross center

Firefighters, with the assistance of a rescue dog, continue looking for victims' bodies in the areas above the day care center at the Alfred P. Murrah Federal Building. A rescue dog found Brandy Liggons, and workers freed her from the rubble so that doctors could provide treatment. She was the last survivor taken out of the building.

and local churches. Had any other people been found? Tensely, people waited to find out.

Stephen Nix was among these anguished people. He waited all night for some word about his wife. At one point, he heard she was in a hospital. But that report turned out to be false. Nix said, "I get pumped up and then I get down. . . . And it's like a roller-coaster all day."[9] Thursday night, the family was still waiting.

In the days after the bombing, people brought dental records and descriptions of loved ones who were still missing. Dentists, fingerprint squads, and X-ray teams tried to match these up to the remains of bodies in the morgue.

Reverend Danny Cavett had an extremely painful job after the bombing. Cavett was the chaplain of Oklahoma City Children's Hospital. People were grieving over their losses and fearful about what would happen to their hospitalized loved ones. Cavett said, "It is their faces that I'll never forget. So much frustration and fear. . . . It is the toughest thing I've ever been through."[10]

No other survivors had been found since the rescue of Brandy Liggons. Still, crews worked on for four days and nights. As Robert Billig prepared to go back Friday night, he said, "You look everywhere and you listen all the time and you hope."[11]

By now, people felt anger as well as grief. Investigations showed that the bomb had exploded from a van parked in front of the federal building. Investigators believed that the bomb weighed around two tons. From the White House, President Bill Clinton issued a statement calling the persons responsible "evil cowards."[12]

On the day of the bombing, one bitter rescue crew painted these words on a brick wall at the bomb site:

We Search for the Truth.
We Seek Justice.
The Courts Require It.
The Victims Cry for It.
And GOD Demands It![13]

"FIND OUT WHO DID THIS"

ANGER AND BITTERNESS spread as people witnessed the intense suffering caused by the bomb. President Bill Clinton told people in Oklahoma City, "We pledge to do all we can to help you heal the injured, to rebuild this city, and to bring to justice those who did this evil."[1]

A firefighter told Oklahoma governor Frank Keating, "Find out who did this."[2]

Oliver (Buck) Revell, a former FBI assistant director, also spoke to the press. He said that this crime would most likely be solved. Revell said, "These people don't realize it, but they're going to leave a trail."[3]

People were now guessing who might have committed this crime. Some blamed foreign terrorists. Many thought that Middle Eastern terrorists were likely suspects. Some people of Arab descent reported being harassed or arrested for questioning. They feared that they might be attacked or even killed.

President Bill Clinton speaks at a prayer service for the victims of the Oklahoma City bombing on April 23, 1995. President Clinton pledged to "bring to justice those who did this evil," and the FBI launched the largest investigation in its history to find the perpetrators.

Other people said an American militia group might be to blame. Militias are nongovernmental, unofficial military groups that have expressed hatred and distrust toward the government. They oppose gun control laws. The Oklahoma City bombing took place exactly two years after the 1993 siege at Waco, Texas. In Waco, federal agents had surrounded buildings where a religious group called Branch Davidians had gathered. The standoff between the Davidians and the agents lasted fifty-one days. On April 19, agents were told to enter the compound to remove illegal weapons and free anyone being held by force.

Army helicopters and tanks arrived. Shots rang out, killing four federal agents. Fires quickly started and swept through the compound. Eighty-five Davidians died, including seventeen children. Militia groups blamed the fires and deaths on the government.

Some militias said the government might have bombed the federal building in order to pin the crime on their groups.

Others guessed that the bomber was a mentally unstable person with no political goal. Still, other people wondered if a drug gang or other criminals had set off the bomb.

The FBI launched the biggest investigation in its history. Within an hour of the bombing, four teams of top agents went to the site. They brought special gear to gather and analyze evidence.

The FBI found important leads the day of the bombing. A cash machine video camera was operating nearby. The camera had recorded an image of a yellow Ryder van parked in front of the federal building just before the explosion.

One agent spotted a valuable clue two blocks away from the federal building. It was a scrap of metal, part of a truck axle. The vehicle identification number (VIN) was still visible. The FBI traced this number and identified the vehicle as a 1993 Ford van. It came from a Ryder rental agency in Junction City, Kansas. Junction City was about 270 miles north of Oklahoma City.

FBI agents were told that two men had rented this van on April 17. The men had used fake names and driver's licenses. Even so, FBI artists gained enough information to make sketches of the suspects.

These suspects became known as John Doe No. 1 and John Doe No. 2. The suspects were both white American males. This terrorism had come from within, not from a foreign country. The FBI offered $2 million for information leading to a conviction.

Two young boys, Kyle Klemp and Ryan Foster, look at the makeshift memorial near the bombed-out Alfred P. Murrah Federal Building on May 3, 1995. People from all over brought flowers, signs, and mementos to the bomb site to honor and remember the victims.

Other agents combed the wreckage. Former FBI director James Fox said, "They are virtually touching every piece of brick and stone and dirt in that crater and putting it through a sifter."[4] They found crystals of ammonium nitrate on pieces of the rental van. It was mixed with fuel oil (racing-car fuel) to make a bomb.

While the FBI gathered evidence, rescue crews found more bodies in the rubble. After that first day, no one else was found alive. More than eight hundred people were being treated for injuries. The death count totaled 168, including nineteen children. Victims ranged in age from four months to seventy-three years old.

Nurse Rebecca Anderson was among the dead. She had been caring for victims when a piece of concrete struck her head. She died four days later. According to her wishes, her heart and kidneys were given to people awaiting organ transplants.

Oklahoma City was in pain. People came to stare at the bomb site. They placed flowers, ribbons, signs, and teddy bears on the chain-link fence that surrounded the area. Resident Mary Jennings said, "Everyone I know has a broken heart."[5]

Sunday was the fifth day after the bombing. A large community prayer service was held at the arena of the Oklahoma State Fairground.

Reverend Billy Graham addressed the mourners. He said, "That blast was like a violent explosion ripping at the heart of America. Long after the rubble is cleared and the rebuilding begins, the scars of this senseless and evil outrage will remain."[6]

Janet Hawkins (right) of Oklahoma City holds her niece, Megan, as they view the memorial outside the Alfred P. Murrah Federal Building. As the community mourned the loss of loved ones, the FBI announced it had taken a suspect into custody.

A TRAIL
OF EVIDENCE

WITHIN DAYS OF THE BOMBING, the FBI announced that they had a suspect in custody. The owner of a motel in Junction City recognized John Doe No. 1. He had stayed at the motel under the name Tim McVeigh.[1] He had signed in on April 14 and checked out on April 18—the day before the bombing.

A computer search revealed that a twenty-seven-year-old man named Timothy McVeigh was in jail in Perry, Oklahoma. McVeigh had been arrested the day of the bombing on unrelated charges. He had posted $500 bail and was scheduled for release in less than an hour.

At 10:20 A.M. on April 19, McVeigh's yellow Mercury Marquis had been stopped about sixty miles north of Oklahoma City. State trooper Charlie Hanger saw that the car had no license plate. He pulled McVeigh over. As the men were talking, Hanger saw a noticeable bulge under McVeigh's jacket. Reaching over, he discovered a semiautomatic pistol. McVeigh also had a five-inch-long knife. Hanger arrested

McVeigh on concealed weapons charges. At that time, police did not connect him with the bombing. McVeigh spent two days at the county jail in Perry, Oklahoma.

The FBI later found a sealed envelope in the car McVeigh had been driving on April 19. Inside were printed materials that criticized the United States government. Sections of some articles were highlighted. One passage discussed the killing of federal workers.

Officer Hanger also gave the FBI a business card McVeigh had left in his patrol car. It was from a military supply company in Wisconsin. On the back, these words had been written: "TNT at $5 a stick. Need more. Call after 01 May. See if you can get some more." McVeigh made no secret of his hatred toward the U.S. government.[2]

Formal charges were filed against McVeigh, and agents went to the Perry jail to take him to federal prison. As they left, angry crowds outside the jail yelled, "Baby-killer!"[3]

The FBI also located a man it thought might be John Doe No. 2. But six weeks after the bombing, he was cleared of suspicion. Rental shop records showed this man had come in a day later.[4]

By then, investigators had turned their attention to Terry Lynn Nichols. On his driver's license, McVeigh had given the address of Terry Nichols's brother James. McVeigh had served with Terry Nichols in the Persian Gulf War. Both men had ties to armed, antigovernment militias.

Reporters claimed that as many as one hundred thousand people throughout the nation belonged to such militias.[5] These groups, often

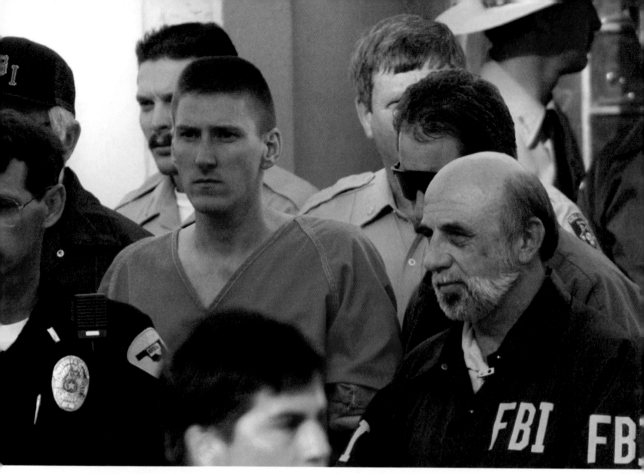

Law enforcement officers escort Timothy McVeigh (in orange jumpsuit) from the Noble County Courthouse in Perry, Oklahoma, on April 21, 1995, to be taken to federal prison.

heavily armed, believe the government has too much control over people's lives. Some also say there is an international conspiracy to destroy or take over America.

With a warrant, FBI agents searched Terry Nichols's farm in Herington, Kansas. They found bomb-making materials and a receipt for ammonium nitrate. This substance had been used to make the Oklahoma City bomb. Neighbors had seen a Ryder truck parked behind Nichols's home two days before the bombing.

Thousands of people gathered at the site of the Oklahoma City bombing on April 19, 1996, one year after the terrorist attack. The names of all the victims were read aloud during the ceremony, and those in attendance honored the memories of those who died with 168 seconds of silence.

In Nichols's basement, agents found blasting caps. They also found a drill bit that matched the marks left on a broken padlock at a nearby quarry. Explosives had been stolen from that quarry several months before the bombing. Inside Nichols's garage were white plastic barrels with blue lids—the same type used in the bombing.

Terry Nichols was arrested. FBI agents questioned him for nine hours. Investigators continued to gather clues. Timothy McVeigh and Terry Nichols were charged with murder, conspiracy, and destruction of government property. All three charges carry the death penalty.

Two seemingly ordinary men were charged with this horrible crime. Newsman Peter Jennings spoke to people who knew Timothy McVeigh. Jennings reported, "Those who had known him most of his life all said the same thing—the Tim McVeigh they knew could not have done it. He was a nice kid, a smart boy. He was the creative one. He was happy. He was friendly."[6]

Yet the government said their case against him was solid.

A memorial service marked the one-year anniversary of the bombing. Some survivors left town that day because their memories were too painful. Thousands of others gathered at the site of the Alfred P. Murrah Federal Building. About six hundred firemen and rescue team members joined them. Many grieving family members and survivors held roses. There were 168 seconds of silence in memory of those who died. The names of the victims were read.

After laying flowers on wreaths, people went to a public memorial service. Oklahoma governor Frank Keating said:

> At 9:02 on the morning of April 19th, 1995, we were together. We are together again today. Ours has been a very difficult journey. . . . I pray that each of us on this day of remembrance will look to our neighbors and remember that out of immense tragedy came an even greater outpouring of good.[7]

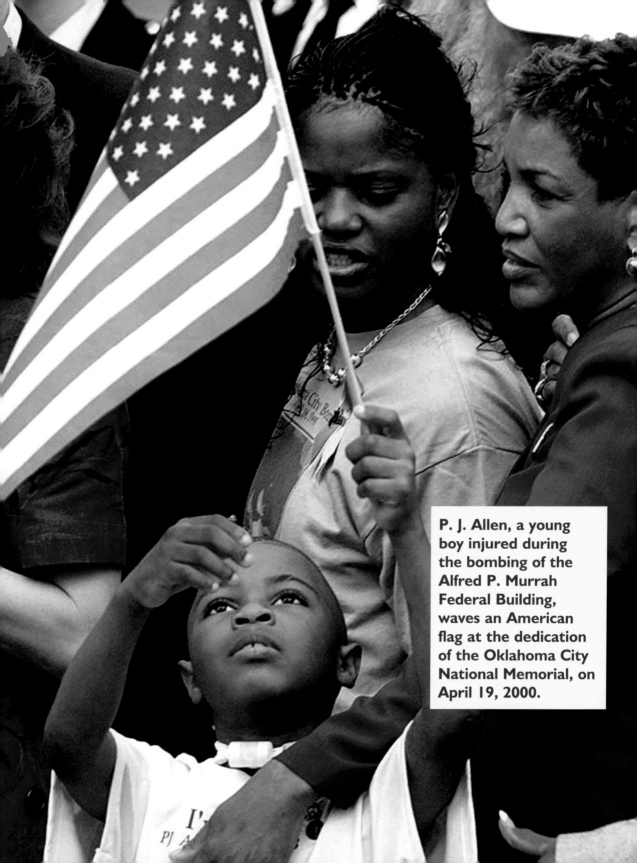

P. J. Allen, a young boy injured during the bombing of the Alfred P. Murrah Federal Building, waves an American flag at the dedication of the Oklahoma City National Memorial, on April 19, 2000.

TERRORISM IN AMERICA

IN JUNE 1997, Timothy McVeigh was found guilty of bombing the federal building in Oklahoma City. A jury of seven women and five men deliberated for twenty-three hours before reaching a decision. He was convicted on all of the eleven charges against him. The charges included conspiracy to use a weapon of mass destruction, destruction of federal property by explosives, and first degree murder.

On the morning of June 17, 2001, McVeigh was executed by the government that he despised. The drugs injected into his right leg first sedated, then poisoned, and finally killed him. He was pronounced dead at 7:14 A.M. McVeigh remained stubbornly unrepentant. He died without offering any kind of apology.

His accomplice, Terry Nichols, was sentenced to life imprisonment without the possibility of parole.

A few months after the horrendous bombing, Oklahoma City Mayor Ron Norick appointed a task force for creating a permanent outdoor memorial, a memorial museum, and a National Memorial Institute for the Prevention of Terrorism. In October 1997, President Bill Clinton signed a law creating the Oklahoma City National Memorial as a part of the National Park Service. The Outdoor Symbolic Memorial was dedicated on April 19, 2000, which was the fifth anniversary of the bombing. The memorial is located where the Alfred P. Murrah Federal Building once stood and it is open to visitors 24 hours a day, 365 days a year.

A reflecting pool, the remaining portions of the Murrah Building, and an American Elm Tree, which survived the bombing, are parts of the memorial. The memorial also features a field filled with 168 empty chairs to represent the empty chairs at the dinner tables of the families of the 168 victims. The chairs are arranged in nine rows to symbolize the nine floors of the destroyed building. Since its opening, the Oklahoma City National Memorial has had more than 4 million visitors.

In the aftermath of the Oklahoma City bombing, the Clinton administration revised a draft of an earlier antiterrorism bill that had been prepared in response to the 1993 bombing of the World Trade Center in New York City. In that terrorist attack, four members of an Islamic extremist group detonated a large bomb. The bomb was placed in the complex's underground parking garage. Six people were killed and over a thousand more were injured.

One of the provisions of the revised bill required that certain chemicals used to manufacture explosives had to be microscopically marked. The microscopic markings would help investigators trace where the components of a chemical had been manufactured or purchased.

The gun lobby vigorously opposed the provision. They said that tagging gunpowder was a form of firearm registration. Their strong opposition led to the provision being changed to a study that would only apply to plastic explosives.

The Clinton administration was able to pass the Antiterrorism and Effective Death Penalty Act of 1996 (AEDPA). The bill had strong

In this photo, the field of chairs at the Oklahoma City National Memorial is seen behind the reflecting pool on September 12, 2011. The 168 chairs represent the empty chairs at the dinner tables of the 168 victims' families.

bipartisan support in both houses of Congress. President Clinton signed the bill into law on April 24, 1996.

The AEDPA was controversial because it had a far-reaching impact on the law of habeas corpus in the United States. The legal term *habeas corpus* is Latin for "you are ordered to have the body." It means that after a person is arrested, a lawyer can obtain a writ of habeas corpus. The writ orders the police to appear in a court of law with the person they arrested. The court then decides if the police have sufficient reason to hold that person in confinement. The purpose of the law is to prevent the wrongful imprisonment of someone accused of a crime.

The legality of the AEDPA was soon challenged because it set strict deadlines for prisoners seeking a writ of habeas corpus and limited their ability to file successive writs.

Defenders of the law said that it prevented frivolous petitions and appeals. Critics of the law said that limiting a person's ability to file multiple appeals made it more likely for an innocent person to be executed. The law was upheld by the United States Supreme Court in the 1997 case of *Felker* v. *Turpin*. In a unanimous decision, the Supreme Court ruled that the limitations placed by the AEDPA did not unconstitutionally suspend the writ of habeas corpus.

After the terrorist attacks of September 11, 2001, another major antiterrorism law was enacted. In October 2001, President George W. Bush signed the Patriot Act into law. The act greatly expanded the powers of law enforcement officers. It gave them the power to detain any noncitizen in the United States who is suspected of posing a threat

The South Tower collapses following the terrorist attack on the World Trade Center on September 11, 2001, in New York City. Following the 9/11 attacks, President George W. Bush signed the Patriot Act into law, greatly expanding the powers of law enforcement.

to American security. The Patriot Act also expanded the power of law enforcement officers to spy on American citizens.

Law officers now have greater freedom to monitor e-mail accounts, conduct wiretaps, and access private data, such as medical records and bank statements. The act has also given law officers easier access to a citizens' library and bookstore records so they can monitor what they have been reading.

In May 2011, President Barack Obama signed a four-year extension for three of the act's major provisions—searches of business records, roving wiretaps, and the conducting of surveillance of individuals who are suspected of terrorist-related activities that aren't linked to any

After the 9/11 terrorist attacks and the passage of the Patriot Act, federal and state governments heightened levels of security across America, especially at airports, harbors, bus and train terminals, and around government buildings. In this photo, passengers go through security checkpoints at Denver International Airport.

terrorist group. Since its enactment, some provisions of the Patriot Act have been ruled unconstitutional in various federal court decisions.

Although the Patriot Act increased levels of security in the United States, there still have been some acts of domestic terrorism in America. While much smaller in scale than the Oklahoma City bombing, the attacks have resulted in property damage and the loss of American lives.

Several of them have been linked to people who subscribe to the beliefs of the sovereign citizen movement.

The FBI has called the movement an "extremist anti-government group." People who call themselves sovereign citizens believe that they are not subject to federal, state, or municipal laws. They also reject most forms of taxation. According to a report by the Southern Poverty Law Center, the movement has approximately three hundred thousand members in the United States and Canada.

"These people just don't respect the badge," said FBI spokesman Stephen Emmett. "There is a potential for violence in them that stems from their extreme philosophy."[1]

While the sovereign citizens are called a movement, they don't have members who pay dues to belong. Nor do they have elected officers who act as spokespeople for the movement. It is more of a philosophy than an actual movement.

Timothy McVeigh's accomplice, Terry Nichols, was a sovereign citizen. In February 2010, Andrew Joseph Stack III, another person linked to the sovereign citizen movement, crashed the plane he was piloting into an Austin, Texas, office building where 190 employees of the U.S. Internal Revenue Service (IRS) were working. The crash killed both Stack and IRS manager Vernon Hunter. Thirteen other people were injured in Stack's suicidal attack.

About three months after Stack's fatal crash, two Arkansas police officers were shot and killed while detaining two sovereign citizens during a traffic stop. Jerry R. Kane and his teenage son, Joseph, were stopped while traveling on an interstate highway outside of West Memphis, Arkansas. While one police officer was attempting to frisk Jerry, Joseph emerged from their minivan and opened fire on the two officers with an AK-47. The Kanes later wounded two more officers in a shoot-out in a Wal-Mart parking lot before they were slain by the police.

Most recently, yet another person linked to the sovereign citizen movement was apprehended for shooting Congresswoman Gabrielle Giffords and eighteen other people at a Tucson, Arizona, shopping plaza. On January 8, 2011, Jared Lee Loughner killed six people and injured fourteen others, including Congresswoman Giffords. Prior to the shooting, Loughner posted videos on YouTube where he articulated some of the beliefs he held that were associated with the sovereign citizen movement.

Loughner has been charged in federal court with multiple counts, including the attempted assassination of a member of Congress and the murder of a federal employee. He is currently being held without bail while awaiting trial.

The Oklahoma City bombing and the terrorist attacks of September 11, 2001, have permanently changed the way Americans live, travel, and interact with their government. There is a heightened level of security and scrutiny in airports, bus and train terminals, in and around government buildings, and at American harbors and ports. Most Americans have willingly accepted this as the price they pay for their nation's safety and security.

CHAPTER NOTES

CHAPTER 1. "THIS ISN'T SUPPOSED TO HAPPEN"

1. Bill Hewitt and Bob Stewart, "April Mourning," *People*, May 15, 1995, p. 101.
2. "Survivors of Oklahoma City Bombing Recall the Day," *Morning Edition With Bob Edwards*, National Public Radio, April 19, 1996.
3. Ibid.
4. Quoted in Richard A. Serrano, "April 19, 1995," *Los Angeles Times Magazine*, Sunday April 13, 1997, p. 16.
5. Ibid.
6. "No Place to Hide," *48 Hours*, CBS News, April 20, 1995, Burelle's Transcripts, p. 3.
7. Quoted in Serrano, p. 14.

CHAPTER 2. HOURS OF AGONY

1. Nancy Gibbs et al., "The Blood of Innocents," *Time*, May 1, 1995, p. 59.
2. Ibid.
3. Ibid.
4. Ibid., p. 62.
5. "Survivors of Oklahoma City Bombing Recall the Day," *Morning Edition With Bob Edwards*, National Public Radio, April 19, 1996.
6. Bob Stewart, "Answers to a Prayer," *People*, May 15, 1995, p. 106.
7. Testimony from the penalty phase of the trial of Timothy McVeigh, quoted in Tom Morganthau and Peter Annin, "Should McVeigh Die?" *Newsweek*, June 16, 1997, p. 22.
8. Linda Kramer, "A Sister's Luck, Another's Loss," *People*, May 15, 1995, pp. 101–102.
9. Gibbs et al., p. 62.
10. Ibid., p. 64.

CHAPTER 3. HOPE AND DESPAIR

1. "No Place to Hide," *48 Hours*, CBS News, April 20, 1995, Burrelle's Transcripts, p. 9.
2. Nancy Gibbs et al., "The Blood of Innocents," *Time*, May 1, 1995, p. 64.
3. "No Place to Hide," p. 9.
4. Gibbs et al., p. 61.
5. Gail Wescott, "The Last Life Saved," *People*, May 15, 1995, p. 104.
6. Gibbs et al., p. 63.
7. Ibid.
8. "The 8-Minute Key to Happiness: Celebrity Inspiration," *Woman's World*, March 5, 1997, p. 9.
9. "No Place to Hide," p. 11.
10. Carlton Stowers, "Healing Spirit," *People*, May 15, 1995, p. 103.
11. John Leland, Debra Rosenberg, and Karen Springen, "I Think About It All the Time," *Newsweek*, May 8, 1995, p. 35.
12. Evan Thomas et al., "Cleverness—and Luck," *Newsweek*, May 1, 1995, p. 30; James Carney, "Measure of a President," *Time*, May 1, 1997, p. 65.
13. Richard A. Serrano, "Two Years Ago, a Bomb Ripped Through the Alfred P. Murrah Federal Building in Oklahoma City," *Los Angeles Times Magazine*, April 13, 1997, p. 16.

CHAPTER 4. "FIND OUT WHO DID THIS"

1. James Carney, "Measure of a President," *Time*, May 1, 1995, p. 65.
2. Nancy Gibbs et al., "The Blood of Innocents," *Time*, May 1, 1995, p. 57.
3. Evan Thomas et al., "Cleverness—and Luck," *Newsweek*, May 1, 1995, p. 31.
4. "No Place to Hide," *48 Hours*, CBS News, April 20, 1995, Burrelle's Transcripts, p. 20.
5. Evan Thomas et al., "The Plot," *Newsweek*, May 8, 1995, p. 34.
6. Quoted in Richard A. Serrano, "April 15, 1995," *Los Angeles Times Magazine*, April 13, 1997, p. 14.

CHAPTER 5. A TRAIL OF EVIDENCE

1. Evan Thomas et al., "Cleverness—and Luck," *Newsweek*, May 1, 1995, p. 34.
2. Richard A. Serrano, "Trooper Testifies on McVeigh's Arrest," *Los Angeles Times*, April 29, 1997, p. A-20.
3. Thomas et al., p. 35.
4. "John Doe Number Two," *Good Morning America*, ABC, May 6, 1997.
5. Tom Morganthau et al., "The View From the Far Right," *Newsweek*, May 1, 1995, p. 36.
6. ABC News Special Report: "Peter Jennings Reporting: Who Is Tim McVeigh?" *ABC News*, 1997.
7. "Voices in the News Last Week," Sunday, *Weekend Edition* with Liane Hanson, National Public Radio, April 21, 1996.

CHAPTER 6. TERRORISM IN AMERICA

1. Michael Braga, "Economic crisis has proved a boon to the sovereign-citizen movement," *Sarasota Herald Tribune*, July 31, 2011, p. 6A.

GLOSSARY

bipartisan—Marked by or involving cooperation, agreement, and compromise between two major political parties. For example, Democrats and Republicans in Congress both supporting the same bill.

militia group—Unofficial, armed military groups whose members express hatred and distrust toward the government.

sovereign citizen movement—A loosely organized collection of groups and individuals who share extreme antigovernment beliefs.

terrorism—The use of violence to frighten, hurt, and kill people in order to gain or maintain political power.

terrorist—A person who uses violence, either toward specific targets or randomly, to achieve political goals.

white supremacist groups—Groups whose members believe that white people are superior to other races. They believe white people should dominate those other races.

FURTHER READING

BOOKS

Brownell, Richard. *The Oklahoma City Bombing*. Detroit: Lucent Books, 2007.

Friedman, Mark. *America's Struggle With Terrorism*. New York: Children's Press, 2011.

Levin, Jack. *Domestic Terrorism*. New York: Chelsea House, 2006.

Paul, Michael. *Oklahoma City and Anti-Government Terrorism*. Milwaukee, Wis.: World Almanac Library, 2006.

Silate, Jennifer. *Terrorist Attack: True Stories of Survival*. New York: Rosen Publishing Group, 2007.

INTERNET ADDRESSES

Federal Bureau of Investigation (FBI): Domestic Terrorism
<http://www.fbi.gov/news/stories/2009/september/domterror_090709>

Oklahoma City National Memorial & Museum
<http://www.oklahomacitynationalmemorial.org/>

The Oklahoma City Bombing and the Trial of Timothy J. McVeigh
<http://law2.umkc.edu/faculty/projects/ftrials/mcveigh/mcveightrial.html>

INDEX